Off the Shelf

In loving memory of Bernard Stone

and The Turret Bookshop

Off the Shelf

A Celebration of Bookshops in Verse

Edited by Carol Ann Duffy

PICADOR

First published 2016 by Picador

This new edition first published 2018 by Picador
an imprint of Pan Macmillan
20 New Wharf Road, London N1 9RR
Associated companies throughout the world
www.panmacmillan.com

ISBN 978-1-5098-9708-7

The publishers are grateful to the following for permission to reproduce copyright material.
Dylan Thomas: 'In my craft or sullen art', from *The Collected Poems of Dylan Thomas:
The Centenary Edition* (Weidenfeld & Nicolson), copyright © The Trustees for the
Copyrights of Dylan Thomas.

Visit www.picador.com to read more about all our books
and to buy them. You will also find features, author interviews and
news of any author events, and you can sign up for e-newsletters
so that you're always first to hear about our new releases.

Contents

Foreword vii

Last Bookshop in Britain – Patience Agbabi 1

Book Learning – Jo Bell 3

Open Book – Rachael Boast 5

Notes on Bookbarn International after a Visit;
with a Questionnaire Answered by O and L – Sean Borodale 7

In Defence of Old Men Dozing in Bookshops – Colette Bryce 12

In a Cardiff Arcade, 1952 – Gillian Clarke 13

Contemporary Americans – Billy Collins 14

MacNaughton's Bookshop – Peter Davidson 15

Beware the Books – Imtiaz Dharker 16

Without Prejudice – Edward Doegar 18

At the Minster Gate Bookshop – Maura Dooley 21

In the Drowned Bookshop – Carol Ann Duffy 22

The Secondhand Bookshop – Ella Duffy 23

Gathering – Ian Duhig 24

River Tigris, River Euphrates – Paul Farley 25

The Bookshop at the End of the World – Vicki Feaver 27

For My Wife, Reading in Bed – John Glenday 29

Lockyer's – Paul Henry 30

The Argument of his Book – Robert Herrick 31

Apotheosis at the Signing Table – Clive James 32

G. & A. Bowden – Alan Jenkins 33

Silver Moon – Jackie Kay 35

Goodbye, Bargain Basement – Neetha Kunaratnam 37

The Wardrobe – Zaffar Kunial 39

We Lay Down a Story – Liz Lefroy 40

Note Taking – Liz Lochhead 41

Bookshops – Michael Longley 44

Blank Page Of First Old Book He Read – Glyn Maxwell 45

What Happens Nest – Helen Mort 47

Booked – Daljit Nagra 48

The Tilt – Mark Pajak 49

Bookshop – Don Paterson 51

The Girl Who Ate Books – Jean Sprackland 52

The Elements of Reading – James Sutherland-Smith 53

The Future of Books – Michael Symmons Roberts 56

Notes on the Art of Poetry – Dylan Thomas 57

Books – Katharine Towers 58

Bookeries – Kit Wright 62

Biographical Notes 65

Foreword

In June 2016, in a fortnight either side of the Referendum, the poets Gillian Clarke, Imtiaz Dharker, Jackie Kay and I travelled from Falmouth to St Andrews, via Wales, on a poetry tour, *Shore to Shore*, to celebrate the UK's Independent Bookshops. At each event, we invited a poet associated with the area to perform alongside us — and were often upstaged. Our aim was to connect with readers, writers and, of course, our heroic booksellers, who are so vital to our communities. To support this venture, Picador published *Off the Shelf*, an anthology of specially commissioned poems about the joys of Bookshops.

On the original tour, we were disappointed not to be able to visit more cities, towns or villages with much-loved local Bookshops — so we made a vow that we would try to add more places another year. So here we are in 2018 — the meaning of Brexit as unclear as it was two years ago — back on the road: this time taking a different route and journeying from Penarth to Dunoon. It seemed an excellent idea to add some extra poems to our original anthology, so this new *Off the Shelf* contains some newly commissioned poems, alongside some old favourites of mine.

My thanks go to Camilla Elworthy and Kish Widyaratna at Picador; to all the poets who will be joining us on the road; to the Independent Bookshops who are helping to make this second venture possible; and, most importantly, Dear Reader, to you.

CAROL ANN DUFFY

Patience Agbabi

LAST BOOKSHOP IN BRITAIN

I won't tell you where it is
or what I did to make the boy talk
but I'll tell you this:

had some gilt-edged Garamont
so close to my chest
I'm in print;

a delivery deadline so dead
its heart stopped.

Someone had surrendered their shed.

Never seen so many rare spines
paper four walls.

I knew my lines
but my tongue
was no match for the man
who'd sat there so long
he read minds.

I blinked too fast.
He read mine

and from under the counterfeit
magicked a white-hot hardback
fresh in its jacket.

You'd die for the smell.

I weighed it in one hand,
let the other braille
the bossed title, like I rehearsed.

Latest edition, he said:
and I handed over the first.

Jo Bell

BOOK LEARNING

For Joe: and for the people of Scarthin Books, Cromford

A boatman don't need letters much.
He knew his payday maths all right
and all the diesel secrets of a Lister HR2
and had the old wet map of Birmingham
well-travelled in the coils of his brain
but books were something new.

He started on the alphabet at sixty-six
as others take up French or watercolours.
Each character a knot, with all the grace of knots;
a line made useful in three loops.
He drove me to the boatyard, reading signs.
S T O K E   O N   T R E N T, he lettered out.

Only fools make fun of scholars. He spoke it
like a latch: the open side hatch of a boat
that lets the true air in to cool the engine.
The M6, clemmed with Eddie Stobart trucks,
became a text; the motorway a manuscript
illuminated by the van of Singh and Sons –

YOU'VE HAD THE COWBOYS – TRY THE INDIANS.
Laughter, and he pocketed those knots of ink,
well on the road to Kerouac, to Rolt and all those names
you read in bookshops: on the road from Gutenberg
to Stoke on Trent, which leads on to a drunken path
and once in twenty years will take you home.

Rachael Boast

OPEN BOOK

Based on the third section of Akhmatova's *The Way of All the Earth*

The smog thickens towards nightfall.
Let Akhmatova walk with me
as far as the corner. A choir
of discord is growing in the city.
Bells ring out and men in the black
of their vocation stand in a line,
holding the line. No one is praying.
This is neither the time, nor the place.
All the stores are open late,
that which was under lock and key
displaced as the choir rises an octave
above plutocracy, the air crackling
with static, with slogan, the Party
Headquarters billowing smoke
from its doorway. I wipe my eyes
and step into the shattered road.
'Here? Is this the place?'
Nothing has been touched.
I wasn't to know that anyone
who presses their face to the glass
would see themselves become sylvan
through an uncommon visage.
A decorated tree is flourishing,

pushing up from under the floor,
ancient and inevitable. A book slips
from its shelf in the branches, landing
at the root, falling open on a page
on which is written the language
of the unspoken. In this silent cache,
time has not been passing.

Sean Borodale

Notes on BookBarn International after a Visit; with a Questionnaire answered by O and L

What did you do, today
between varnished wooden shelves, gridded, maze-like?
How old are you?
      Twelve.
      Eight.
Why did you want to come here?
      To find.
      To play.

The stored honeypot is here
and page pollen, adventure by subject:
biography, astronomy, Palaeolithic. Spores that will mushroom
up through the understorey from darkness in elf cup red.
To look for what is hidden in books;
we scan the tree shade of catalogues
in these shared hours, hear whispers behind stacks.
We are separated by years of shelves.

Absorbed bound, printed paper;
xylophone of spines,
names like tuning forks
are the names of rivers in our forests.

On the banks of a shelf,
books as stepping stones
to sunlight in barcode; transaction gold.

We think with scansion
how, shelved in such huge volume,
the isolated, active book for each of us sleeps like larvae.

Lorca
Tragedies

Guns of Massacre Gap
by Walter A. Tomkins
Price 25p

The (big) Cat Encyclopaedia.

You have found a gripping tale of violence in cattle towns.
What do you like?
        Vivid language.
You have found a book of cats.
What do you like?
        Kittens, like moths.

My book is as quiet as fat or flour.
New price: 50p.

Some shelving is out of bounds,
an inner sanctum battery of select-energy-books: for sale worldwide.
A pond in the woods. Require the rights.
Not everything is lost,
all used book sale now gives trace
royalty back to its author.
The forest breathes in this way,
re-lives out of afterlife;
insulated, physical, warmth through page-turned silence.
Because reading is air.
Word sinks into body, body into word, no?

    It was my birthday, we came to this bookshop, this bookbarn.
    It was my brother's birthday.
At what height did you search?
    Any height I could get to.
    If I couldn't reach I climbed up the shelves
    to a good looking book at the very top.
    A book like a lost world.
    The things you can see from the height of a book.
What did you find?
    A postcard of someone in 1962
    on holiday in Sussex.
    Treasure, problems, a letter, probably
    of a skeleton now,
    beautiful flower pressed against
    the word Linnaeus flat as an insect.

People don't know what's left when they die in a book.
   But the old book
could have been left in a library where
no one read books
where in the old days someone stuffed a postcard between
   the pages
thinking it was a post box into the future.
I am a future.
Horrible cuttings with smudged print.
Design for a bridge on a scrap of paper.
Could you have stayed for long?
   Rest of my life.
   Not overnight, or slept in a ton of pages,
   a bookshelf pigeon in a nest like at home.
What does it smell of?
   Bookdust.
   Dust.
What do used books feel like?
   Keys to the centre of the earth.
   Rough, smooth, slightly warm.
   Cold, if they haven't been read.
Could you feel a history?
   From the battered corners,
   some must have been thrown or chafed along a wall.
   I got an odd feeling from one, falling
   through my thumbs.
What is a book like that's never been read?
   Full of a secret.

Do you think it is good to recycle books?

    It's another chance to change a life.

    No. You can't read a book that's been recycled.

Is it like treasure?

    Better than treasure.

    Some is like sport, not like team sport:

    everyone shouting at you to pass the ball.

Can you describe it?

    A barn for those without homes at the moment.

    A flat-packed statue of mind-bending information.

    An aura of page turns.

What could be better?

    We saw a man selecting a length of old Penguin Paperbacks,
        all in orange.

    Some brighter, some darker.

    He went out with just the middle section of a tiger.

Was that his criteria?

    Love of books.

    He'll be back,

    for the head and the tail.

Colette Bryce

IN DEFENCE OF OLD MEN DOZING IN BOOKSHOPS

from *The Observations of Aleksandr Svetlov*

There are days I drop in on Mikhail at the shop
when time will diminish like flour tap-tapped
through a sieve. I position myself at the window
and open a volume, selected at random
but normally fiction (for the window seat
is very well placed for the longest lies).
Having polished my glasses, I then proceed
to read and absorb the opening sentence.
For example: *During a small-bow contest
one of the archers coughs.* Isn't that odd?
I turn it over, open again, and feast my eyes

on the termination: *'It is premature
to speak of Autumn', she replied,
'yet I feel myself ascending
nine times towards you in the night'.*
Now what would you make of that?
Indeed. So consider that old 'has-been'
who seems to be dozing in a spot of sun;
he may be, in truth, in the act of applying
the logic derived from a lifetime of dying
to the problem of what could have possibly happened
in between.

Gillian Clarke

In a Cardiff Arcade, 1952

One of those little shops too small
for the worlds they hold, where words
that sing you to sleep, stories
that stalk your dreams,
open like golden windows in a wall.

One small room leads to another,
the first bright-windowed on the street,
alluring, luminous. The other is dusk,
walled with pressed pages, old books
with leathery breath and freckled leaves.

What stays is not the book alone
but where you took it down,
how it felt in your hands,
how she wrapped it in brown paper,
how you carried it home,

how it holds wild seas
that knock the earth apart,
how words burn, freeze,
to break and heal your heart.

Billy Collins

CONTEMPORARY AMERICANS

I was trying to make my way
across a busy street in San Francisco,
when I thought of the new anthology of poetry
I'd been flipping through earlier that morning
with my pot of tea and two pieces of cinnamon toast,
and how I ended up wedged between James Tate and Bob Dylan
because the poets were arranged, old to young, according to age.

I had to avoid a couple of cars,
cross over two sets of trolley tracks,
and dodge a guy on a bicycle with a ski cap
in order to get across the street and enter
one of the city's many little welcoming parks
with their hedges and benches and shade trees
and often a juggler, girls on a blanket, an old man doing tai-chi.

And that's where I lay down on the soft grass,
closed my eyes, and after a little while
began to picture the three of us all lined up in a row
according to the editor's wishes,
sliding out of our mothers in order, one after the other,
then ending up pressed together on a shelf
in a corner bookstore, yodeling away in the dark.

Peter Davidson

MacNaughtan's Bookshop

Exigent spinster mistress Edinburgh,
Thin wind-bride with your stone-cold mural crown,
What consolations hold your votaries?
Rigours and ironies, microcosms of books.
This shop's the city in epitome:
Modest in elegance, reticent in grace
Of curving windows and of cut stone stairs;
And the dim labyrinth of books within
Cases of histories and biographies;
Antiquities in folio behind glass.
The back room full of shelves and shelves of Scotland:
Rivers and moors, topographies long gone,
The reasoned pleasures of dead advocates,
The garden darkened by the elder trees.
Let us patrol the New Town squares at dusk:
Unshuttered windows, distance-coloured walls
Painted rain grey, smoke green, or ashy rose,
And lamplight thrown on rows and rows of books.
The frost descends on streets of libraries,
These freezing precincts of enlightenment
Are holding for the moment, just, they hold.

Imtiaz Dharker

BEWARE THE BOOKS

Mad-dog mid-day snarls off the bumper to bumper
eyeball to eyeball hand on the horn buffalo-hide
son-of-a-donkey dick-of-a-dog fucker-of-sister
roadwar at Horniman roundabout. You step aside

from the roar on the street to the door
of Strand Book Stall. Outside falls away.
The air stands still for one beat, heat drops
like a coat, but if you expect a safe haven

think again, you are mistaken. You feel it
at once, the catch in the throat, the prickling
under the skin that says danger lives here,
and you want it.

This was what you came for,
wasn't it, my dear?

You lift your head for the scent of it. You hear
a ruffling, then a page turns and roars,
blows a girl off a shelf and flings her
across the world to become something more

than she thinks, more than herself.
A faint rustle is all the warning you have before
a tiger springs. Do you feel its breath in your face?
Out of a bookcase, armies of children come

marching to the beat of a drum made of tin,
an entire civilization tumbles down stairs,
and there, a philosopher dares to argue with God
fighting thunder and lightning with words.

Behind you, time shuts down.
Against the palm of your hand, a spine is rippling,
something dangerous prickling under the skin,
and you want it. This was what you came for

my dear, wasn't it? Come in.
Hold it to your heart like a ticking thing.

Edward Doegar

WITHOUT PREJUDICE

Charleston, SC: 2002

Nabokov turns his back on Joyce
to examine his glasses – in focus, out of fashion.
Identified by legend, he wears a fur hat
like a patronym. This is the coffee-shop-section
of Barnes & Noble. It is populated
with wallpaper posters. Langston Hughes is more blue
than black; handsomely generic, he almost resembles
a namesake. The two Eliots are obvious:
she sports an androgynous pink bow-tie; he's predatory
restraint. Dorothy Parker's name-tag would fit
any other woman, hatted and single.

Under the Influences the fluorescence yawns . . .
Nothing happens. The air-conditioning curses us
under its breath. Books are arranged like convenient props
in a warehouse theatre: we're stage-lit – strip-lit –
but somehow still in the wings waiting to burst
onto the scene of our lives . . .
                                        Over-exposed,
there's no 'we' to speak of, each of us a fortress
of possessions: books hoarded from the stacks,
colonies of paper. An aproned barista-cum-waitress
patrols the space between us disinterestedly

like the UN. Every table is an island
with its own provision of sugar-free alternatives:
one sachet is two servings; the problem of waste
is ever-present. Self-help encroaches on philosophy.

I turn my attention back to the book
I've read before, setting aside the thick editions
of worthy frontiers for second helpings
of *A Moveable Feast*. At the periphery of my mind's eye
a pee-shy Fitzgerald worries about his Zelda
having an imagination. Miss Stein's bedroom voice
comes over the tannoy. Ford Madox Ford, that vain walrus,
is quarrelsome and stinks. Ancient gossip provides
the restorative escapism of another era.
But as I close the covers I meet the disappointment
of progress, discovering myself here killing time
in this overly clean overly well-lighted place.

*

The present lapses into the past, so I must relive
what I thought then, what I thought
without thinking. How I'd learnt to read someone's haircut
as their political beliefs, their clothes as a desire
to be desired. I don't remember the people I saw,
I remember what I saw them as:
a limp handshake, cornrows, a dental plan . . .
I had that tell-tale preference for a balanced argument,
playing devil's advocate for any Lost Cause.
Even now I want to weigh in on my own behalf,
cite youth and ignorance as reasonable doubt,

as if this was about me, as if guilt was just
a personal matter, a means of expression: mea culpa.

But our thoughts and feelings are never only our own.
I've played Papa's part, bearded and unbearded.
I know we can't become what we pretend to be
but was the pretending me? I craved the simple surety
of hindsight as much as the silly macho control
of prose. I *was* that self-composed American in Paris,
not some mongrel Brit in the States. I believed myself
to be white.
                Listen to me! I'm still borrowing
someone else's language, still borrowing an identity,
a passport for the travel of fiction. But being moved
by writing can no longer mean safe passage.
Orwell meets my eyes as I lower them to the table.
He looks out from a Barnes & Noble mug,
the faded souvenir of that winter abroad.
I re-read him recently, his *Down and Out*, and realized,
for the first time, that he was anti-Semitic,
or that he had been, then, when he wrote it.
And I must teach myself not to treat this as a lesson.

Maura Dooley

AT THE MINSTER GATE BOOKSHOP

for Nigel Wallace

Our spring crocuses were slim spines of green and orange,
our blue skies Hoggart, Hobsbaum, Laing, Ford,
autumn came with the sound of turning leaves
and winter brought a crowd to warm their hands
or sometimes steal. The Emily Dickinson thief had made
herself a coat of felt in which to slip the Roberts
edition, *Ivory boards. Top-edge gilt. Near fine.* Vivaldi
or Bach soothed the fraying nerves of King Penguin
hunters, signed First collectors, Saturday browsers
or students rummaging for Hobbes or Jung. Rackhams
and Dulacs, rested their *only slightly rubbed* shoulders
but everywhere Garamond outfoxed us all in buckram,
Morocco, velvet or vellum which yet could barely hold
that flock of words – wild words! – that roar of words.

Carol Ann Duffy

In The Drowned Bookshop

Inhoop, Inhospitable, Inhospitality,
Inhuman: lacking kindness, pity or compassion;
cruel, indifferent – a dictionary drifts, open at *I*.
I beg to differ.

        An A to Z of Mammals, spoiled
sinks. Not human, the beached whales of Skegness.
Nor the river, perused though it has each poem,
Biography, Once Upon A Time . . .

                Poor tomes;
nothing to be learned from them by the human inhuman.

In splashes the tardy Minister for Floods, smart
despite cheap new wellingtons, austere.
There bobs *Mary I of England, 1516–1558;*
Calais written on her heart.

Ella Duffy

THE SECONDHAND BOOKSHOP

where books, lifted from cardboard caskets,
rest in rows; each aisle a ward

for booksellers to tend to torn spines,
coffee-bruised pages,

ten till six; when visitors call on the
not-yet-discharged

or bring those, bandaged in newspaper,
home to unwrap

onto new shelves until, settled, their
tender wounds heal into scars.

Ian Duhig

GATHERING

'Anthology' means 'a gathering of flowers':
broke, I'd find seeds in an old Shelter shop
where I never got what I came for but more,

charitable even unto its shelvers' latitude,
Religion hosting Farmer's *Jesus on Mars*,
the Baking section Swan's *Desert Mothers*;

Crime had a tea-leaf-reading guide with tips
such as Darjeeling's easier on ageing eyes,
discourage clients from dunking your biscuits,

how when you have bad news, don't sugar it,
but pour them out more tea and let them dunk.
A whole order of magic destroyed by teabags.

I can see a future for one copy of our anthology,
misplanted under Gardening in a charity shop,
its leaves yellowing unseen in dusty desert air;

a puzzled, green-fingered customer picks it up:
it sprays open like a magician's paper bouquet.
One flower catches her eye. She reads it, smiling.

Paul Farley

RIVER TIGRIS, RIVER EUPHRATES

Standing small before armor-plated books
as big as cardboard stooks but made of lead

on twin steel shelves, in a gallery, in the Eighties,
whatever the artist meant, or meant to explore,

you read them as a monument to your Eighties,
this decade that sags in the middle with the weight

of homelessness, or homelessness of the sofa-surfing
kind, lost down the sofa divide of London

with the coins and hairclips, lost in the seat structure
of the city, where the surfer's call to arms—

Can I crash at yours?—is heard, then a world of bookshelves
—planks from skips on pillars of house bricks—

that you'd read rather than read the books themselves,
hiding from history, safe at the source

of civilization most nights, then being woke
by bin men, light through nailed-up drapes, the morning

news—the reactor burned, the ferry listed to port—
and the world tilted. You never made your bed

[25]

in cardboard—things never got that heavy—and you'll turn
the page before the decade is out, and rooms

are being forgotten, flickering, lit by tea lights,
where bookshelves loomed and looked over you most nights.

Vicki Feaver

THE BOOKSHOP AT THE END OF THE WORLD

Everything stopped: ferries, planes,
radio signals, the internet, electricity,
and any news of what was happening.
Food was the priority: inshore fishing
and working crofts and vegetable plots.

I reopened the shop: not to sell books
but to satisfy a hunger for the stories
and the history of the world as it was.
All were welcome – children with scrubbed
hands – to sit at the table and read.

Smell of whale oil and melting tallow.
Soft light from lamps and candles
shining on shelves filled with tattered,
broken-spined books, and on people
squeezed on benches and the floor.

Some have travelled miles – a few
on rickety bicycles, but most walking –
to hear the island's poets and singers:
Hamish's lament for the missing geese
whose ravelling and unravelling skeins

heralded autumn – his mouth organ's
harsh chords echoing their hoarse cries;
Murdo's ballad about the rich retirees
who, when the Co-op shelves emptied,
their money worthless, jumped from cliffs;

Mary's elegy for the whales –
wandering lost and bewildered
through strangely changed oceans,
stranded on beaches – whose blubber
we plunder to light our dark winters;

Caitlin's celebration of the flowers,
still pushing through mingled peat
and wind-blown sand to embroider
the machair: wild yellow pansies,
storksbill, milkwort and eyebright.

My poem tells of how as a child
I looked up at the stars shining
in the immensity of black space
and wondered if people like us
were living on a far-away planet.

Now, I wonder if the crew
of a spaceship orbiting the earth
at night, would see the glimmer
of our lights, and other lights,
or if the rest of the globe is in darkness.

John Glenday

FOR MY WIFE, READING IN BED

I know we're living through all the dark we can afford.
Thank goodness, then, for this moment's light

and you, holding the night at bay – a hint of frown,
those focussed hands, that open book.

I'll match your inward quiet, breath for breath.
What else do we have but words and their absences

to bind and unfasten the knotwork of the heart;
to remind us how mutual and alone we are, how tiny

and significant? Whatever it is you are reading now
my love, read on. Our lives depend on it.

Paul Henry

LOCKYER'S

The door's cowbell, tall Cyril
ushering, his own bookmark
between 'Roses' and 'Churchill',
the fey assistant's Bakelite . . .

The floorboards creaked in 'Poetry'.
A branch scratched the skylight.

I could hear my sons in the park,
sometimes recognized a cry,
a soul's baroque latticework
annotating *The Waste Land*.

The books we almost bought
were precious in our hands –

Keyes's *The Iron Laurel*,
a pocket Tennyson, inscribed
For Olive, before I sail . . .

Weekends turned, chimed.
The boys grew tall enough
to panic a cowbell, drag me home

as Mr Lockyer's century closed
on a park's empty shelves,
a room full of leaves.

Robert Herrick

THE ARGUMENT OF HIS BOOK

I sing of brooks, of blossoms, birds, and bowers,
Of April, May, of June, and July flowers.
I sing of May-poles, hock-carts, wassails, wakes,
Of bridegrooms, brides, and of their bridal-cakes.
I write of youth, of love, and have access
By these to sing of cleanly wantonness.
I sing of dews, of rains, and piece by piece
Of balm, of oil, of spice, and ambergris.
I sing of Time's trans-shifting; and I write
How roses first came red, and lilies white.
I write of groves, of twilights, and I sing
The court of Mab, and of the fairy king.
I write of Hell; I sing (and ever shall)
Of Heaven, and hope to have it after all.

Clive James

APOTHEOSIS AT THE SIGNING TABLE

Looking ahead for places to sit down,
Come spring I might, one last time, limp downtown
And into Heffers, into Waterstones,
In either order, haul my creaking bones,
To stand, with a long-practised half-lost look,
Somewhere beside the stack of my new book
Until I'm asked to sign. As if surprised
I'll sit down, slowly, seeming paralysed
By sheer humility as they bring stock
Of books that I forgot I wrote. I'll sign
Each tempting title-page with my by-line
Like a machine for hours on end. The clock
Will seem not to exist. My signature
Will grow, however, steadily less sure,
Until, the felt-tip quivering in my grasp,
I scrawl the hieroglyphs of my last gasp.
A final short sip from my cup of tea
And I will topple, croaking tragically.
Slumped on the carpet, I will look around,
And all the walls of books in the background,
More splendid even than they were before,
Will seem to hear my small voice from the floor.
'Heffers or Waterstones, this is goodbye,
But I rejoice that I came here to die,
So one day those who know my books may say
That this is where he signed his life away.'

Alan Jenkins

G. & A. Bowden

The window-display's a window
In G. & A. Bowden, Bookshop.
A note says the owner's a widow
And the bookselling had to stop,

The book-buying and the catalogues
And the salesmen who dropped by.
The business side went to the dogs.
The stock went to Hay-on-Wye

And bare boards shine where I'd rehearse
One of my adolescent selves,
'A strange child with a taste for verse',
Sheepishly, among the shelves

Of Poetry . . .The knowing smile,
Tweed skirt and cardigan she wore,
The lady who owned it then! A style
That went with Art, post-war,

And Literature; her husband's pipe-smoke
Competing with the smell of paperbacks.
To me, it smelt of safety. Now I choke
On empty walls, the lack of stacks,

And everything that's gone with them
(It must be that). Not far away
The river ebbs and flows, the rhythm
That means life. Or so they say.

Jackie Kay

Silver Moon

Your names, old records, *Court and Spark*, *Dark Side of the Moon*,
A shop window welcome; open hands, new friends.
A wintery evening, nights drawing in. Warm glow:
Sisterwrite, *Compendium*, *Silver Moon*.

How you grew up reading nights to dawn.
Books you found only here, the then unknowns:
Audre Lorde, Nikki Giovanni, Toni Cade Bambara;
The Bluest Eye held up a haunting mirror, Pecola Breedlove.

Switched lights on; eyes wide open – *Sula*, *Corregidora*
You read and read with wonder: *We Are Everywhere:*
Writings About Lesbian Parents! Or *A Raisin in the Sun.*
Voices from Women's Liberation, Maya, Djuna, Zora,

The Spinster and Her Enemies! Or Lucille Clifton.
And by the silvery light of the bookshop you grew up
By the open door, standing alone, together,
Other readers as engrossed, browsing, basking –

The blessed benevolence, the sweet, sweet ambience
Of independent bookshops, remember Thins!
Look how you still love their names: Voltaire and Rousseau,
Grassroots, books gathering and honing your years:

Black and white striped spines, tiny irons, Viragos, Shebas,
The distinct spiral on the cover of your old *The Bell Jar*
Your skin's pages; your heart's ink, your brain's Word Power:
Jamaica Kincaid, Bessie Head, Claribel Alegría

Don't let them turn the lights out, dears.
Keep them safe, New Beacons, shining stars,
Look how you've aged with your beloved books, dear hearts.
Keep coming in, keep the bookshop door ajar.

Neetha Kunaratnam

GOODBYE, BARGAIN BASEMENT

For David on his 80th birthday

We shuffle down this cramped aisle,
pore over its warped shelves,
and thumb these paperbacks
arranged in their guesswork of genres.

There's nostalgia in these peeling walls,
witness to our casual quests,
as we've scoured second-hand philosophies,
or flirted with fictions hyped beyond us.

For old time's sake we try to divine
a reading order from the riddle
of these creased spines: *The Hours, Mrs Dalloway,*
The Postpartum Husband, On Suicide.

And I squat over the plastic crates,
seeking one more fable for Amber,
risking paper cuts as I rifle through
the misdeeds of cartoon pigs and cats.

Heavy with our last haul, we leave
mouthing farewells, and fast-forward weeks
to see the whitened weft of cobwebs,
and the thick air yearning to be exorcised.

We will feel the lure of the bookstore in town,
its refurbished cafe and brand new floors,
happy that Amber can scamper like a zephyr
in its wide expanse. And you'll nurse a coffee,

sunk deep in a sofa, delving at leisure into
The Better Angels of Our Nature, while I'll slip away
to skim through the unread verse
in the basement of neglected bargains.

Zaffar Kunial

THE WARDROBE

might be a good name for a bookshop, small but oddly ongoing,
the kind you'd happen upon, and enter, perhaps alone, perhaps
not, in a long grown-up coat. And as you place your cold hand
in its gloveless pocket and feel the tweed edges of empty space
you might be reminded – as I am – of a sleeved scene in a book;
a scene I knew firstly from a VHS film I'd replay, by the fire, rapt
as a kid, watching Lucy's cartoon fingers push through long fur
coats – further, touching branches. Snow. I don't know about you
but I never forgot this feeling I've never had – like that episode
of sleeplessness in a book I did read later, spellbound, where a fir
branch, tapping a gusty window, was never fir, but skin and bone;
Cathy's icy ghost hand: *I'm come home.* Gripped, gripping, through

the broken glass. On top of the MDF wardrobe near the landing
fittingly high from the ground, was our family's Quran, wrapped
in cloth. Gilt-edged, wide enough to house three scripts. Around
the time I'd be glued to films like *The Lion, the Witch* . . . I'd place
a chair beneath, take down the shrouded weight, undo the black
sleeve, open a page and read a corridor of the English that slept
in the margins. I wasn't sure why I did this, or what I'd fear
I might miss, or if I was sitting right, or how to truly feel through
to the words. I'd lift them back, rewrapped, on the wardrobe.
Distantly, I've long looked up to books. The distance they cover.
Picture me, delayed, walking through a bookshop – say this one
– forgetting what I first came in for, or if I ever really knew.

[39]

Liz Lefroy

WE LAY DOWN A STORY

When we return to the hotel you agree to rest
but only for so long. The rain is darkening the windows
and I know I want to keep you here.

It's around three o'clock – I settle beside you on the bed.
You're so comfortable, wearing your dark blue jersey:
I feel no real need of the city any more.

Liking the sound of your voice, I say, 'Read to me,'
take out the book you bought me, pass it to you,
though I don't think you'd imagined it like this.

The sounds of this afternoon lay down a stillness:
the far-below thrum of cars, rain falling against glass,
your reading easing out the time we have left till dusk.

Liz Lochhead

ESSENTIALS

Saturday morning in the little independent bookshop
in the wee row of shops across the road and
there's a boy at the very serious business of deciding
how to spend his two tenth-birthday book-tokens,
there's a baby crawling underfoot whose mother's
a little too engrossed for now
in what she's picked off the shelves to bother
about the baby or the baby's big sister who's
pulling all the big and bright and beautiful books,
each peach pear plum,
from the bottom shelf of the children's section and
– under the watchful but indulgent eye of the proprietor –
turning pages, pointing out all her favourite characters
to her imaginary friend.

These books are her real friends and she knows it.

This man does too. He's just selected three new ones,
is paying with his card.

They don't do coffee here.
They sell books.
Oh, a few cards (it's only a wee bookshop) art
reproductions 'blank for your greeting'
suitable for birthdays, sympathy or thank-you notes,
a row of budget-label classical CDs

— a new Saturday-morning symphony perhaps?
Here's a selection of DVDs of old Hollywood
black-and-white movies — that couple who look as if
they've only recently uncoupled (her hands
in the back pockets of his jeans) are choosing their
own old favourites to share with each other soon
and he pecks her on the cheek to celebrate her
each eccentric choice.

There's a woman
looking for a book she doesn't know what it's called or
who wrote it but it was a foreign name and
they were talking about it on the radio this morning on
a programme the proprietor won't have heard
because she was probably busy opening up the shop
at that time and no she can't really remember
what it was about but it sounded
an essential read.
A minute or two later, bit of
trial and error, the proprietor has identified it
and is ringing up a sale.

What am I doing in here?
I only popped out for essentials.
And my book-bag has only netted half a dozen eggs,
one of those nice sourdough loaves and
the weekend *Guardian* from the corner-shop next door
but, as usual, something's pulled me in.

There's a new display —
a whole shelf of brand new paperback editions

of every book ever written
by my favourite living author.
I seize upon it, scrabbling, eager to discover a
new book by her I haven't read yet, but
of course there isn't one – evidently
my favourite author, now she's over eighty
has, thus far, stuck to her rumoured resolve
not to publish another collection of stories –
these dozen volumes contain nothing I don't
know by heart in hardback, but this, this is a
New Selected, this would be portable for travelling
and it is a lovely cover . . .

At the till the proprietor tells me
one of the books I have on order has come in,
though the other is still reprinting
but she's hopeful.
So am I.

Michael Longley

BOOKSHOPS

Mullan's in Royal Avenue, Erskine Mayne's
Close to the City Hall, dusty corridors,
Aisles of books, elbow room and no more,
Our first pamphlets jostling for attention,

Then first slim volumes (if nobody's looking
I'll move mine to the front. Nobody's looking).
Death of a Naturalist, Late but in Earnest,
Night-crossing, No Continuing City –

The terrible shock of our names and titles.
Each wee bookshop has closed, a lost cathedral
With its stained-glass window that depicts
A young poet opening his book of poems.

Glyn Maxwell

Blank Page Of First Old Book He Read

I don't know who he is but by his skin
so freckly-pink
     when mine's so worn and yellow
he's new to this, so new he brings me in
     and meets me with his nostrils.

While those two are his eyes his eyes are wells
so brown and deep
     a drop will drop forever
look, this is the dawn of somewhere else,
     his little mouth is opening

its O of sunrise as if every day
there is to come
     might catch him knowing nothing.
Light will climb with him, time have its say
     when the small voice is ready

and only then, now all the air is breath
until it's quiet.
     Soon his eyes aligning
bob along my furrows, tread the earth,
     the ginger head in tow now,

the soft indignant brow becoming clear.
I've bided here
    so long I've quite forgotten
what he encounters, what he's learning there –
    three memories stay with me:

his grin away and back again as if
he'd found somewhere
    we both belonged, the turning
I took for love and, when time called enough,
    light narrowing so gently.

Helen Mort

What Happens Next

The thing with novels is they always end.
I lose my thread, forget my place. The book
falls shut. I'm inarticulate again
though I'm the one who's making all this up.
I try to sound well-read, express myself
through plots: *Stoner* and *Nineteen Eighty-Four*.
I gesture with conviction to the shelf.
My life's a chapter out of Richard Ford

where someone's always driving out of town
thinking about a chance they missed, an ex,
a doomed encounter in the snow, profoundly
necking Scotch . . . You frown. What happens next?
I've an idea I don't know how to write.
I hold the page to you, set it alight.

Daljit Nagra

BOOKED

Gone for lack of a song *Paradise Lost*
and *The Riverside Shakespeare*. Gone
in the swing of a bulldozer Balzac, Quixote,
Jane Eyre, Wuthering Heights and Goethe.
Never to be seen if not read *The Brothers
Karamazov, War and Peace* and *Finnegans Wake*.
Gone too Galileo, Einstein and Anne Frank,
along with Plato and all the faiths in a black hole
to languish with the lavish prints from Michelangelo,
Monet, Kahlo or the scores of Mozart. Gone
in a butchery the kiddie corner with cushions
for *Where the Wild Things Are, The Tiger
Who Came to Tea*, Potter, Beaker, Grimm.
Gone too the chance to be lit by chance
by a snuck-away shelf of contemporary verse,
and all the hand-me-down lore that defines us.
Overnight and dead to the world in a swamp urge
Astronomy, Horror, Biography, Health and Humour.
Which is how it feels when the range of human time,
one more house of books leaves a high street!

Mark Pajak

THE TILT

Those days when mum's hangover
was a dark kitchen, sat at the table,
head in her hands like a full bowl,

I'd slip out of the house and come here;
this bookshop on Luke Street.
In here I could shut the world

with a door and be walled in
by hardbacks, boxes of dead leaves.
Paperbacks neat as piano keys.

In here it was quiet. Floorboards
tense as a frozen lake. The book
in my chest that opened and closed.

And I'd kneel to a low shelf,
choose at random and break open
a loaf of paper. It didn't matter

that I couldn't afford it, or soon
the owner would make me leave,
or that I was only four and couldn't read.

The smell of an old book is a memory of trees.
A boy can tilt into it, the way a drunk
tilts her glass, and lean back emptied.

Don Paterson

BOOKSHOP

```
bbbbbbbbbbbbbbbbbbbbbbbbbbbbbbbbbdbbbbbbbbb
ooooooooooooooooooooooooooooooooooooooooooo
ooooooooooooooooooooooooooooooooooooooooooo
kkkkkkkkkkkkkkkkkkkkkkkkkkkkkkkkkrkkkkkkkkk
bbbbbbbbbbbbbbbbbbbbbbbbbbbbbbbbbbbbbbbbbbb
ooooooooooooooooooooooooooooooooooooooooooo
ooooooooooooooooooooooooooooooooooooooooooo
kkkkkkkkkkkkkkkkkkkkkkkkkkkkkkkkkkkkkkkkkkk
bookbook                              bookbook
bookbook                              bookbook
bookbook                              bookbook
bookbook                              bookbook
bookbook                              bookbook
bookbook                              bookbook
bookbook                              bookbook
bookbook                              bookbook
bookbook                              bookbook
bookbook                              bookbook
bookbook                              bookbook
bookbook                              bookbook
bookbook                              bookbook
bookbook                              bookbook
bookbook                              bookbook
bookbook                              bookbook
bookbook                              bookbook
bookbook                              bookbook
bbbbbbbbbbbbbbbbbbbbbbbbbbbbbbbbbbbbbbbbbbb
ooooooooooooooooooooooooooooooooooooooooooo
ooooooooooooooooooooooooooooooooooooooooooo
kkkkkkkkkkkkkkkkkkkkkkkkkkkkkkkkkkkkkkkkkkk
```

Jean Sprackland

THE GIRL WHO ATE BOOKS

It started with hymn books. In school assembly
she would lick her favourite page, 'Jerusalem the Golden':
sleek and translucent, milk and honey.
The teacher said it was unhygienic.
Besides, he said, this was India paper, a gift of God,
making bibles and hymn-books light enough for missionaries
to carry into all the dark corners of the world.

But it didn't stop there. Soon she was eating holes
in *Elidor*, *Little House on the Prairie*, *Stig of the Dump*.
She still gets hungry in bookshops, recalling the juice
and the grain of it. She grew insatiable, even for thicker,
rough-cut stuff. She would chew on *Real Life Maths*
or *People and Places*, then spit out grey pellets
fit only for flicking at boys' necks.

The teacher sighed and said she should have more respect.
He said that a thousand years before paper came to England
the Chinese made it from bark and fishing nets.
He said that medieval monks wrote on the soft white skins
of stillborn calves, and how would she like to eat that?

James Sutherland-Smith

THE ELEMENTS OF READING

Water

You become exotic in bookshops,
An odd fish shimmering among reefs of words,
Grazing between varieties of coral,
Nose deep, your nourishment invisible.
The element of water might not seem
To be present. Yet hold an endpaper
Of even a bestseller to the light
And you'll see not blankness but ghosts,
Fragments of fibres that once drew water up
Into leaf and blossom. Then open the book
And you, too, will absorb from the aquifer
Of humour, thought and feeling that's inside.
The tritest blurbs carry more than a hint;
It brought tears to my eyes. I laughed till I cried.

Fire

You switch on a torch, light a candle,
Hold a taper before you enter the dark
Or open books, all of which are kinds of fire
That illuminate the mind, melt the heart.
Second-hand bookshops can be warm places
When you take shelter out of the rain

And come across a copy of a book you've read,
Mislaid and never thought you'd find again.
Past pleasures flare until you see the name
Of another scrawled inside. An old flame
Has moved on as you must along the rows
Seeking to replace what kept you up all night.
It's a mystery tale where you follow your nose
While on the shelves new passions ignite.

Earth

Animal, vegetable, mineral;
Not as heavy as a stone or a brick,
But solid material that will endure
While readers and the life of the mind exist.
Just touch an ancient edition, leather bound,
Quartos of hand-made paper, dandy rolled
For text and quality illustration,
Iron in the printer's ink, not in the soul.
The complex smell of a book is a flower bed
In the very early morning. Breathe it in
Like Stanley Baldwin sniffing the wild, lush
Prose of his latest Mary Webb, *Gone to Earth*
In a dull debate on a finance bill.
These days Honourable Members play Candy Crush.

Air

She ran a lifestyle bookshop which didn't stock
My immediate choice of a good read,

But vegan recipes, eco-plumbing,
A tear-jerker, *Forgive the Gentle Weed*.
She wore a blue embroidered muslin blouse
Through which her flawless skin seemed to glow.
Had she anything on medieval cuisine?
She searched her database and answered No.
Did I have an alternative in mind?
I thought that such a slender girl must live on air
As just then a breeze rattled the blind
And turned the pages of the book she kept there.
So it was with a feeling of dismay
That I glimpsed the title, *Fifty Shades of Grey*.

Spirit

There's a traditional clink or chime of a bell,
A welcome mat that buzzes when we step
Eagerly inside or a modern swish
As double doors slide back to reveal
People of all ages, not a crowd,
Lifting books from shelves and tables, thumbing
Pages with the occasional whisper,
Comment, frown or Oh look! at what they read.
Elsewhere in supermarkets there may be books
In shiny wrappers whose sell-by-date
Is hardly any longer than packs of chicken breasts.
But here is a cave of plenty not merchandise.
Here is the means for what we might not credit
Is possible in this life: paradise.

Michael Symmons Roberts

THE FUTURE OF BOOKS

Or this: some sci-fi aeon where a drill
draws out a deep core sample,
a candy stick of sands and clays,
each civilization, the gist of all its stories,
packed into a slab of sediment.
Our slice has its own distinctive shade and scent
– paper-musk, the dark behind bookshelves –
but it so mystifies our future selves
they fry it like black pudding, a salt and bitter
jus of atlas, sonnet, gossip, scripture.
Text is long gone, adrift in virtual vaults
with mislaid passcodes. Think of bottles
on a cyber-tide, never breaking shore,
bearing love letters for strangers.

Dylan Thomas

NOTES ON THE ART OF POETRY

I could never have dreamt that there were such goings-on
in the world between the covers of books,
such sandstorms and ice blasts of words,
such staggering peace, such enormous laughter,
such and so many blinding bright lights,
splashing all over the pages
in a million bits and pieces
all of which were words, words, words,
and each of which were alive forever
in its own delight and glory and oddity and light.

Katharine Towers

BOOKS

after Larkin

If I were called in
to construct a religion
I should make use of books.

Going to church
would entail a bracing traipse
through make-believe woods.

My liturgy would employ
a splendour of lamplight
and the hush-hush of pages at dusk.

And I should be the old
factotum of books,
bent to the beautiful spines
and mouthing the words like a moth.

Kit Wright

BOOKERIES

They're often NEW AND SECOND-HAND
These days and it's the second-hand
That turns back time. When I was small,
Round-eyed with wonder, I'd ascend
Behind my father stairs that creaked
In buildings wholly occupied
By books and books. A bookery
Would be a fit name for their roost:
Also, the minor crooning sounds
Of satisfaction and surprise
The customers emitted seemed
A woodland strain of sorts. I passed
Old leather bindings, some as frail
As earthen river-cliffs, while some
Gleamed in their umber garrisons
With gold-leaf medals on broad chests.
Both powder blue and faded rose
Were singing colours on the decks,
The landings and the terraces,
In standing coffins, catafalques
Of books and books and books. I duly
Followed the coconut matting road –
Or trail of lino, threadbare cloth –
The mealy, malty, nutty, dusty

Scent of reading till we found
The denizen within his den:
His coins in a tobacco tin,
His notes elastic-banded. There,
A small transaction. So outside
And sweets for me. And then the bus,
On which my father tried the weight
And character of those *trouvailles*
Which gave new wings to his pursuit,
The riches of a modest man.

Biographical Notes

Patience Agbabi is a dynamic poet, performer and Fellow in Creative Writing at Oxford Brookes University. She read English at Oxford and has an MA in Creative Writing from Sussex. Patience has spent twenty-five years celebrating the written and spoken word. She's on the Council of Management for Arvon. Canterbury Laureate from 2009 to 2010, she received a Grant for the Arts to write a contemporary version of *The Canterbury Tales*. This fourth poetry collection, *Telling Tales* (Canongate, 2014), was shortlisted for the 2014 Ted Hughes Award for New Work in Poetry, and Wales Book of the Year 2015.

www.patienceagbabi.wordpress.com

Jo Bell is a poet, teacher and outspoken advocate. She is widely published and has been the director of National Poetry Day, the Canal Laureate for the UK and the instigator of award-winning global poetry workshop, the 52 Project. Her latest collection, *Kith*, and the bestselling workbook, *52: Write a Poem a Week*, are both published by Nine Arches Press. She lives on a narrowboat on the English waterways. For poetry news follow her on Twitter @Jo_Bell. Find out more at www.jobell.org.uk.

Rachael Boast was born in 1975. *Sidereal* (Picador, 2011) was longlisted for the *Guardian* First Book Award and won the Forward Prize for Best First Collection, and the Seamus Heaney Centre for Poetry Prize. She edited *The Echoing Gallery: Bristol Poets and Art in the City* (Redcliffe Press). *Pilgrim's Flower* (Picador, 2013) was shortlisted for the Griffin Prize. A third collection, *Void Studies*, is published in November 2016. She lives in Bristol.

Sean Borodale works as a poet and artist, making scriptive and documentary poems written on location. His first collection of poetry, *Bee Journal*, was shortlisted for the Costa Poetry Award and the T. S. Eliot Prize. His documentary poem *Mighty Beast* was produced for BBC Radio 3's 'Between the Ears' and won the 2014 Radio Academy Gold Award for Best Feature or Documentary. He is a 2014 Next Generation Poet.

Colette Bryce grew up in Derry, Northern Ireland. She lived for some years in London before moving to Scotland in 2002 and later to the North of England, where she now works as a freelance writer. Her most recent collection, *The Whole and Rain-domed Universe* (2014), was shortlisted for the Costa, Forward and Roehampton poetry prizes. From 2009 to 2013 she was Poetry Editor at *Poetry London*. She received the Cholmondeley Award in 2010.

Gillian Clarke, National Poet of Wales 2008–2016, was awarded the Queen's Gold Medal for Poetry in December 2010 and the Wilfred Owen Award in 2012. Her books include a writer's journal, *At the Source*, and her recent poetry collection, *Ice*, which was shortlisted for the T. S. Eliot Prize 2012. A new Selected Poems is published by Picador in 2016. She has written for radio and theatre, and translated poetry and prose from Welsh. *The Gathering/Yr Helfa*, written for the National Theatre of Wales, was performed on the foothills of Snowdon in September, 2014.

Billy Collins has received fellowships from the New York Foundation for the Arts, the National Endowment for the Arts and the Guggenheim Foundation. A professor of English at Lehman College, he was appointed Poet Laureate of the United States for 2001–2003. He lives with his wife in Westchester County, NY.

Peter Davidson is a Fellow of Campion Hall, University of Oxford. He has published a collection with Carcanet, *The Palace of Oblivion* (2008); a book of essays about northern places, *Distance and Memory*, and two cultural histories, *The Idea of North* (2005, new edition 2016), and

The Last of the Light: about Twilight (2015). He lives in Edinburgh and Oxford.

Imtiaz Dharker is a poet, artist and documentary film-maker. Awarded the Queen's Gold Medal for Poetry in 2014, recipient of the Cholmondeley Award and a Fellow of the Royal Society of Literature, her most recent collection is *Over the Moon* (Bloodaxe). With Poetry Live! she reads to over 25,000 students a year.

Edward Doegar's poems, translations and reviews have appeared in various magazines, including *Poetry Review, Poetry London, Prac Crit* and *Poetry Ireland Review*. He's a fellow of The Complete Works programme for diversity in British poetry, and six of his poems are featured in the Bloodaxe anthology, *Ten: The New Wave*. He is the general manager of The Poetry Society and an assistant editor at *The Rialto*.

Maura Dooley's latest collection of poems is called *The Silvering* (2016). In 2015 she was writer-in-residence at the Jane Austen House Museum, Chawton, where she wrote poems published as the pamphlet *A Quire of Paper*. She teaches at Goldsmiths, University of London, and is a Fellow of the Royal Society of Literature.

Carol Ann Duffy lives in Manchester, where she is Professor and Creative Director of the Writing School at Manchester Metropolitan University. She has written for both children and adults, and her poetry has received many awards, including the Signal Prize for Children's Verse, the Whitbread, Forward and T. S. Eliot Prizes, and the Lannan and E. M. Forster Prize in America. She was appointed Poet Laureate in 2009. In 2011 *The Bees* won the Costa Poetry Award, and in 2012 she won the PEN Pinter Prize. She was appointed DBE in 2015.

Ella Duffy is a London-based poet and actor. Her work is being published in the autumn 2018 issue of the *Poetry Salzburg Review*. She is a former Foyle Young Poet who has since collaborated with the Poetry Society, working with students and young poets. She is also the co-founder of bind, an online platform which raises climate change awareness through creativity.

Ian Duhig is a former homelessness worker whose seventh book, *The Blind Roadmaker*, is a PBS Spring Recommendation. A Cholmondeley Award recipient and Fellow of the Royal Society of Literature, Duhig is also a joint winner of a Shirley Jackson Award for short stories, and the only outright winner of the National Poetry Competition, twice. He has been shortlisted three times for the T. S. Eliot Prize. He is currently working on a project involving refugees suffering from PTSD, and their therapists.

Paul Farley was born in Liverpool in 1965 and studied at the Chelsea School of Art. He has published four collections of poetry with Picador, most recently *The Dark Film* (2012). His other books include *Edgelands* (with Michael Symmons Roberts, 2011), and he has also edited a selection of John Clare's poetry. A Fellow of the Royal Society of Literature and a frequent broadcaster, he has received numerous awards including *Sunday Times* Young Writer of the Year, the Whitbread Poetry Prize and the E. M. Forster Award from the American Academy of Arts and Letters.

Vicki Feaver's collection of poems *The Handless Maiden* (Cape 1994, reprinted 2009) won her a Heineman Prize and a Cholmondeley Award. *The Book of Blood* (Cape, 2006) was shortlisted for the Costa and Forward prizes. Her poem 'Judith' won the Forward Prize for the Best Single Poem. Her most recent poems appear in *Second Wind* (Saltire 2015), authored jointly with Douglas Dunn and Diana Hendry. A new solo collection,

I want! I want!, is almost complete. She lives in Dunsyre, a village on the edge of the Pentlands in South Lanarkshire, and in Leith, Edinburgh.

John Glenday was born in Broughty Ferry in 1952. His first collection, *The Apple Ghost*, won a Scottish Arts Council Book Award and his second, *Undark*, was a Poetry Book Society Recommendation, as was his third, *Grain*. He lives in Cawdor, and works for NHS Highland as an addictions counsellor.

Paul Henry was born in Aberystwyth and was originally a songwriter. *The Brittle Sea: New & Selected Poems*, and *Boy Running*, his sixth collection, were recently reprinted by Seren. He has read and performed his work widely, both in the UK and abroad. A Writing Fellow at the University of South Wales, he has presented arts programmes for BBC Radio 3 and 4.   www.paulhenrywales.co.uk

Robert Herrick (1591–1674) was a poet and clergyman. 'The Argument of his Book' begins the collection of lyrical poetry of the same name, which celebrated English country life and his Christian faith.

Laura Jackson (1901–1991) was a poet as well as a critic, writer of novels, short stories and essays, and a lexicographer. Her *Collected Poems* were published in 1938 (revised edition 2001) and among her posthumous works is *The Person I Am* (2011), her memoirs.

Clive James is the author of more than forty books. As well as essays, he has published collections of literary and television criticism, travel writing, verse and novels, plus five volumes of autobiography, *Unreliable Memoirs, Falling Towards England, May Week Was In June, North Face of Soho* and *The Blaze of Obscurity*. As a television performer he appeared regularly for both the BBC and ITV, most notably as writer and presenter

[67]

of the 'Postcard' series of travel documentaries. His translation of Dante's *The Divine Comedy* and his 2015 collection, *Sentenced to Life,* were both *Sunday Times* top-ten bestsellers. In 1992 he was made a Member of the Order of Australia and in 2003 he was awarded the Philip Hodgins Memorial Medal for literature. He holds honorary doctorates from the universities of Sydney, East Anglia and Essex. In 2012 he was appointed CBE and in 2013 an Officer of the Order of Australia. For more information, please visit his website www.clivejames.com.

Alan Jenkins was born in 1955 and has lived for most of his life in London. His collections of poetry include, most recently, *Revenants* (2013), *Paper-Money Lyrics* and, with John Kinsella, *Marine* (both 2015). He is Deputy Editor and Poetry Editor of *The Times Literary Supplement* and a Fellow of the Royal Society of Literature.

Jackie Kay was born in Edinburgh. She is a poet, novelist and writer of short stories and has enjoyed great acclaim for her work for both adults and children. She has published three collections of stories with Picador, *Why Don't You Stop Talking, Wish I Was Here*, and *Reality, Reality*; a poetry collection, *Fiere*; and most recently her memoir, *Red Dust Road*. She is Professor of Creative Writing at Newcastle University, and lives in Manchester, where she is currently Chancellor of the University of Salford. In 2016, she was appointed the new Makar, the National Poet of Scotland.

Neetha Kunaratnam is a teacher. Born in London, he now lives in rural East Sussex with his wife and daughter.

Zaffar Kunial was born in Birmingham and lives in Hebden Bridge. His debut pamphlet was published by Faber & Faber in 2014 as part of the Faber New Poets series.

Liz Lefroy won the 2011 Roy Fisher Prize resulting in the publication of *Pretending the Weather*. Her 2014 pamphlet, *Mending The Ordinary*, is published by Fair Acre Press.

Liz Lochhead, poet and playwright, was until recently Scotland's Makar, or National Poet, a role she enjoyed for the five years of its fixed term. Far from retiring though, Liz is currently putting the finishing touches to her new collection of poems, *Fugitive Colours*, her new play, *Thon Man Moliere*, at the Royal Lyceum Theatre, Edinburgh, and her CD *The Light Comes Back* with indie group The Hazey Janes and saxophonist Steve Kettley. All due out in May and June 2016. Liz recently received the Queen's Gold Medal for Poetry.

Michael Longley was born in Belfast in 1939 and educated at the Royal Belfast Academical Institution and Trinity College Dublin where he read Classics. He has published ten collections of poetry, including *Gorse Fires* (1991) which won the Whitbread Poetry Award; *The Weather in Japan* (2000) which won the Hawthornden Prize, the T. S. Eliot Prize and the *Irish Times* Poetry Prize; and *The Stairwell* which won the Griffin International Prize for Poetic Excellence. His *Collected Poems* was published in 2006. In 2001 he received the Queen's Gold Medal for Poetry, and in 2003 the Wilfred Owen Award. He was awarded a CBE in 2010. He was Ireland Professor of Poetry, 2007–2010. He and his wife, the critic Edna Longley, live and work in Belfast. In 2015 he was made a Freeman of the City.

Glyn Maxwell has won several awards for his poetry, including the Somerset Maugham Prize, the E. M. Forster Prize from the American Academy of Arts and Letters and the Geoffrey Faber Memorial Prize. His work has been shortlisted for the Whitbread, Forward and T. S. Eliot Prizes. Many of his plays have been staged in the UK and USA, including *The Lifeblood*, which won British Theatre Guide's 'Best Play' Award at the Edinburgh Fringe in 2004, and *Liberty*, which premiered at Shakespeare's Globe in 2008. He recently published *On Poetry*, a general reader's guide to the craft.

Helen Mort was born in Sheffield. Her first collection, *Division Street*, was published by Chatto & Windus in 2013 and won the Fenton Aldeburgh Prize. She is a former Poet in Residence at The Wordsworth Trust, Grasmere, and was Derbyshire's Poet Laureate from 2013–2015.

Daljit Nagra was born and raised in West London and Sheffield and has an Indian background. His three collections of poetry have been published by Faber and Faber. He has won the Forward Prize for Best Poem with *Look We Have Coming to Dover!* This was also the title of his first collection, which won the Forward Prize for Best First Collection and *The South Bank Show* Decibel Award. His subsequent two collections have both been nominated for the T. S. Eliot Prize. He is currently Radio 4 and 4 Extra's Poet in Residence.

Mark Pajak was born in Merseyside. His work has been published in *Ink, Sweat & Tears*, *Magma* and *The Rialto*, been shortlisted for the Bridport Prize, highly commended by Buzzwords Cheltenham Poetry Competition and The Poetry Society's National Poetry Competition. His first pamphlet, *Spitting Distance*, will be published by smith|doorstop in late 2016.

Don Paterson was born in Dundee. He works as a writer, editor and musician and teaches at the University of St Andrews.

Burton Raffel was Professor Emeritus of English at the University of Louisiana at Lafayette, and was well known as a translator from Old and

Middle English and other languages. He was also a poet, critic and script-writer.

Jean Sprackland's collection *Tilt* won the Costa Poetry Award, and her most recent collection, *Sleeping Keys*, was published in 2013. She is also the author of *Strands: A Year of Discoveries on the Beach*, winner of the Portico Prize for Non-Fiction. Jean is Academic Director of the Writing School at Manchester Metropolitan University, and Chair of the Poetry Archive.

James Sutherland-Smith was born in Aberdeen, Scotland, in 1948 and is a lecturer in British Cultural Studies in the Institute of English and American Studies at Prešov University, in Prešov, where he has lived since 1989. He has published six full collections of his poetry, the last being his poem cycle, *Mouth*, published by Shearsman Books in 2014. He has translated a number of Slovak poets into English for which work he received the Hviezdoslav Prize in 2003. In 2014 he was awarded the Zlatko Krasni Prize at the Smederevo Poetry Festival for his translations of the Serbian poet Ivana Milankov, and a *Selected Poems* of Miodrag Pavlović was published by Salt Publications in 2014. This year he will publish a selection of the poems of the Slovak poet Ján Gavura, under the title *The Other Monk*, and *Multiple Visions*, a textbook for university students on the theory of Cultural Studies, and in 2017 a selection from the poetry of Mária Ferenčuhová.

Michael Symmons Roberts has published six collections of poetry and received a number of accolades including the Forward Prize, the Costa Poetry Prize and the Whitbread Poetry Award. He is a regular broadcaster and writer for radio, and his work as a librettist has been performed in venues across the world. He is Professor of Poetry at Manchester University and a Fellow of the Royal Society of Literature. His *Selected Poems* is published by Cape in 2016.

Dylan Thomas (1914–1953) was a poet, playwright, scriptwriter and broadcaster, perhaps most famous for his radio 'play for voices', *Under Milk Wood* (1954).

Katharine Towers was born in London in 1961 and read Modern Languages at St Hilda's College, Oxford. She has an MA in Writing from Newcastle University. Her pamphlet 'Slow Time' was published by Mews Press in 2005 and her poems have appeared in publications including *Mslexia* and *The North*. She lives in the Peak District with her husband and two daughters.

Kit Wright is a journeyman bard living in East London. His verse has won several prizes, including the Geoffrey Faber Memorial Prize, the Alice Hunt Bartlett Prize, the Royal Society of Literature's Heinemann Award and the Hawthornden Prize for Literature. His latest collection is *Ode to Didcot Power Station* (Bloodaxe, 2014) and he is completing *Torpedo Justice*.

This anthology of new work by some of our best contemporary poets was published to coincide with the Poet Laureate's Shore to Shore tour of independent bookshops in June 2016. Accompanied by the former National Poet of Wales, Gillian Clarke, Scots Makar, Jackie Kay, and Imtiaz Dharker, recipient of the Queen's Gold Medal for Poetry, the tour travelled from Falmouth to St Andrews, giving poetry readings in such diverse venues as Carlisle Cathedral, the Savoy Theatre, and St Boswells Village Hall, supporting and highlighting the local bookshops and adding a poet associated with each place along the way. These guest poets included: Penny Shuttle, Rosie Bailey, Jane Griffiths, Bernard O'Donoghue, Jonathan Edwards, Paul Henry, Liz Lefroy, Jonathan Davidson, Ifor Ap Glyn, Michael Symmons Roberts, Jacob Polley, Gillian Allnutt, Liz Lochhead, Vicki Feaver and Robert Crawford.